What Am I?

looking through shapes
at apples and grapes

by N.N. Charles

illustrated by Leo & Diane Dillon

THE BLUE SKY PRESS

An Imprint of Scholastic Inc. • New York

For Leo, Diane, and Lee
with thanks
—N.N.C.

For Bon
—L. & D.D.

The Blue Sky Press

Text copyright © 1994 by N.N. Charles
Illustrations copyright © 1994 by Leo and Diane Dillon

For information regarding permission, please write to:
Permissions Department,
The Blue Sky Press, an imprint of Scholastic Inc.,
555 Broadway, New York, New York 10012

The Blue Sky Press is a trademark of Scholastic Inc.

Library of Congress Cataloging-in-Publication Data
Charles, N.N.
What am I?: looking through shapes at apples and grapes/
N.N. Charles; illustrated by Leo and Diane Dillon.
p.   cm.
Summary: Illustrations with cut-out shapes and
rhyming questions introduce fruits, colors, and shapes.
ISBN 0-590-47891-5
1. Toy and movable books—Specimens.
[1. Fruit 2. Color. 3. Shape. 4. Toy and movable books.]
I. Dillon, Leo, ill. II. Dillon, Diane, ill. III. Title
PZ7.D5797Wh   1994   [E]–dc20   93-48835   CIP   AC
12 11 10 9 8 7 6 5 4 3 2 1   4 5 6 7 8 9/9
Printed in Singapore

First printing, September 10, 1994

Production supervision by Angela Biola
Art direction by Kathleen Westray
Designed by Leo and Diane Dillon

I'm red, I'm green,
I'm purple, too —
I'm yellow, orange,
brown, and blue.
I come in shades
of every hue;
I'm tasty, fresh,
and good for you.
This book is just
a simple game:
First look through shapes,
then guess my name.

What am I?

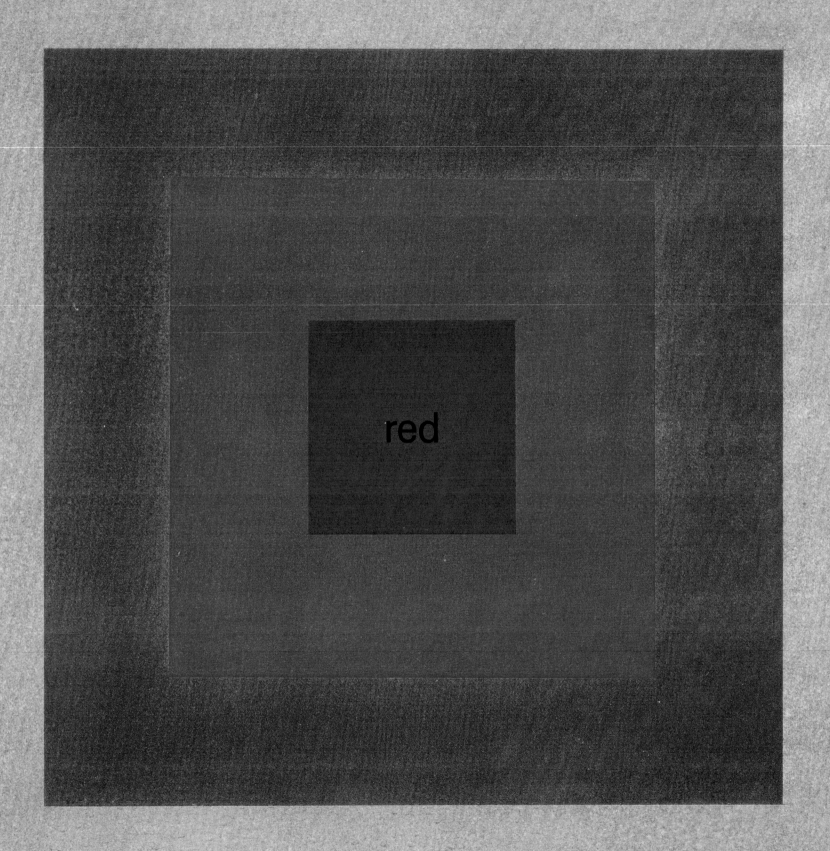

square

I'm red, I'm round,
I fall to the ground.

What am I?

an apple

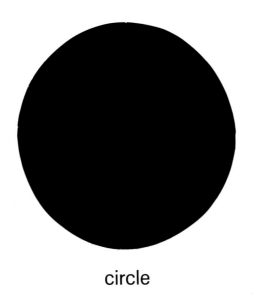

circle

I'm orange, I'm sweet to drink or eat.

What am I?

an orange

yellow

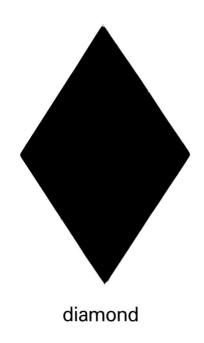

diamond

I'm yellow, I'm thin,
you peel my skin.

What am I?

a banana

green

I'm green, I'm nice
to eat by the slice.

What am I?

an avocado

ngle

I'm blue, I'm small,
I'm shaped like a ball.

What am I?

a blueberry

trian

a grape

I'm red and yellow, blue and green,
and shades of colors in between.

What am I?

hexagon

In nature, there will always be
a rainbow in the things you see.

In places here, and foreign lands,
the rainbow can be seen in hands
that make the world a better place —
a rainbow of the human race.

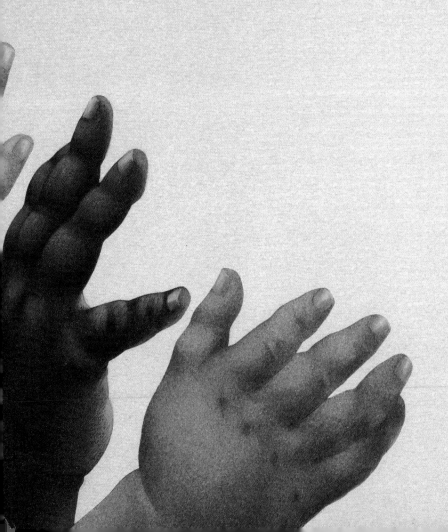